THE PARK IN THE CITY

The Park in the City

by PHILIP RESSNER

photographs by BILL BINZEN

 E. P. DUTTON & CO., INC. NEW YORK

Published simultaneously in Canada by Clarke,
Irwin & Company Limited, Toronto and Vancouver

SBN: 0-525-36620-2
Library of Congress Catalog Card Number: 77-133111

Typography by Hilda Scott
Printed in the U.S.A.
First Edition

For Simon, Alice, and Anabel

In the park, in the middle of the city, the grass and trees grow the way they once did where the buildings are now. The park is the city the way it was before it became a city.

In the cool morning the wind hisses in the leaves
and the park streams with air like ribbons.

The lake winds in and out around the lowest parts
of the park and goes nowhere.

In the winter it shivers in the wind.

In the big field voices disappear into the sky,

but under the stone bridges every sound comes back,
comes back.

In the spring in the park the cool air smells warm.

The old bandstand
is like a porch without a house; the new one

is like a big cup tipped sideways in the grass.

In the zoo the seals look at the people;
the lions and bears look out at the trees.

Up close the earth smells like night and radishes. Under the grass the bugs are busy in the only world they know.

In some places no buildings can be
seen and no people, and the old trees
have no more to say to each other.

The horses have their own road
and look proud of it as they pass.

In the summer the carousel
in the park groans and
twangles. In the winter it
is closed and quiet.

Inside some carousel
horses have leaped high
and stopped; they won't
come down until spring.

In the fall the air
smells like cool fires. The dry leaves lie on the
ground like old letters sent long ago by the spring.

At the boathouse the rowboats float together
like peapods on the water.

In the winter the trees at the top of the hills are wire in the sky, and the grass shines pale as ginger ale.

Right after the snowstorm the big meadow is smooth as
a bowl of sugar with two trees growing in the middle.

At dusk the grass is green as glass.

On the very steep hills your legs run
without trying, and you can't stop.

When the wind blows hard the trees
rock and thrash and try to get away.

In the deep grass the narrow dirt paths
run this way and that like busy dogs.

The paths were made by people
walking here long ago. They will be
here as long as people use them.

ABOUT THE AUTHOR

Philip Ressner loves the city and its life. He is the author of the Dutton title *At Night,* à text and photograph book for children about the city between dusk and dawn. He has also written *Jerome, August Explains,* and *Dudley Pippin.* Mr. Ressner is an editor for a New York textbook publisher and lives in Brooklyn with his wife and three children.

ABOUT THE PHOTOGRAPHER

Bill Binzen has written and illustrated with photographs several books of his own, including *Miguel's Mountain, Carmen,* and *Punch and Jonathan.* He is also a successful advertising photographer. Mr. Binzen is married and has four children.

ABOUT THE BOOK

The photographs were taken during a period of nine months in various parks in Manhattan, Brooklyn, and Staten Island.

The book title is set in Chisel type and the text typeface is Photo Musica. The book is printed by offset.